Facebook

Portal TV

User Manual

The Complete Illustrated, Practical Guide with Tips & Tricks to Maximizing your Portal TV

Gilbert J. Kearns

Copyright © 2020 by Gilbert J. Kearns - All rights reserved.

All other copyrights & trademarks are the properties of their respective owners; Reproduction of any part of this book without the permission of the copyright owners is illegal-except with the inclusion of brief quotes in a review of the work.

Contents

Introduction 1

    What do I need to set up my Portal TV? 2

    What comes with my Portal TV? 2

    How do I set up my Portal TV? 3

    How do I add or remove accounts on my Portal TV? 6

    How does calling work on Portal TV? 10

    How do I turn the camera and microphone off on my Portal TV? 13

    How do I make group calls on my Portal TV? 14

    How do I use AR Effects during a call on my Portal TV? 15

    How do I use Story Time on my Portal TV? 16

    How do I connect or disconnect Alexa on my Portal TV? 18

    How do I use my Portal TV remote? 19

    How do I connect my WhatsApp account to my Portal TV? 21

How do I view regulatory information about my Portal TV? 22

How do I add or remove Favorites from my Portal TV? 22

How do I set up or change the Wi-Fi network on my Portal TV? 24

How do I put my Portal TV in "sleep" mode? 26

How do I pair my Portal TV remote? 27

How do I pair my new Portal TV remote? 28

I'm having trouble with my Portal TV remote. 29

How do I factory reset my Portal TV? 30

How do I use Portal safely with kids in my home? 31

How do I know if my contacts are available to call on my Portal? 32

What is Mic Drop on Portal TV? 32

How do I control the camera during a call on my Portal TV? 33

How do I hide a suggested or recent contact on Portal TV? 34

How do I create or edit a custom nickname on Portal TV? 35

How do I change the Call Settings on my Portal TV? 36

How do I call someone using their Facebook relationship name or nickname? 37

Who can I call or receive calls from on Portal? ... 38

Why am I being asked to log in to my Portal again? 40

Why do I have to log in with Facebook to view or edit certain settings on my Portal? 40

How do I change the language settings on my Portal TV? 42

How does HDMI-CEC work on Portal TV? 43

How do I control audio settings on my Portal TV? 44

How do I adjust the accessibility settings on my Portal TV? 46

How do I update the software on my Portal? 47

How do I connect my Portal to a TV, computer monitor or Ethernet?` 48

How do I set up or change the Wi-Fi network on my Portal TV? 50

How do I adjust Superframe settings on my Portal TV? 51

How do I add or remove photos from Superframe on my Portal TV? 52

How do I manage Superframe photos using the Portal app? 54

How can I add photos to Superframe that I don't want to share on Facebook? 55

How do I manage the apps on my Portal TV? 57

How do I connect my Spotify, Pandora or iHeartRadio accounts to Portal TV? 59

How do I connect Bluetooth devices to my Portal TV? 61

Can I go live on Facebook using my Portal? 62

How do I set up a passcode for my Portal TV? 63

What do the lights on my Portal TV mean? 64

How do I remove an account from Portal remotely? 65

Does Portal have parental controls? 66

How do I take care of my Portal? 67

What information is collected for "Hey Portal"? ... 69

How does "Hey Portal" work with other voice services? 70

How long do you keep my "Hey Portal" voice interactions? 70

Can other people using my Portal see and access my voice interactions and settings? 71

Do you share my 'Hey Portal' voice requests with anyone else? 72

How do you use my 'Hey Portal' voice interactions? 72

Does Portal record all of my conversations? How do I know when Portal is recording? 73

How does "Hey Portal" work? 74

How do I control how Portal handles my voice interactions? 74

How do I use voice interactions with my Portal? . 76

Hey Portal' and Alexa don't understand me 79

Introduction

Facebook's Portal TV is a camera that turns your television into a giant video chat display. It's compatible with both Messenger and WhatsApp, and features an AI-powered camera that automatically pans and zooms to keep you in frame. The large TV screen and wide field-of-view make for a great video chat experience. If both parties have a Portal TV, they can watch videos together, though it only works with Facebook Watch for now. But you can't share songs like you can on the standalone Portals, it lacks a few core apps and it takes up an HDMI port.

There are many other factors that make up the overall goodness of the device. We got a chance at handling the device and we are presenting our User Guide to help you maximize your Facebook Portal Mini.

What do I need to set up my Portal TV?

To set up your Portal TV, you need the following:

- Your Portal TV
- Your Portal TV remote (batteries are included)
- A TV
- An HDMI cable
- A Facebook account or WhatsApp account
- A high-speed, wireless internet connection

What comes with my Portal TV?

Before you set up your Portal TV, make sure you have all the items that should be included in your Portal TV box.

The following items should be included in your Portal TV box:

- Portal TV.
- Remote Control (with 2 AAA batteries inside).
- Power cord.
- Portal TV Quick Start Guide.

Notes:

- A high-speed HDMI cable is not included in your Portal TV box, but Portal TV requires a high-speed HDMI cable for use.
- A high-speed HDMI cable is sold separately.

How do I set up my Portal TV?

Plug in your Portal TV:

1. Plug in the HDMI cable and power adapter, then connect the power adapter to a power source. Your Portal TV will turn on automatically.
2. Plug the HDMI cable into an input on your TV. For best results use HDMI 1.
3. Turn on your TV and select the input.

Find the right place for your Portal TV:

Your Portal TV may be mounted on top of your TV or placed on a flat surface underneath. Avoid placing your Portal TV directly on top of a speaker, too close to a speaker, directly on top of a sound bar or too close to a sound bar.

Mount your Portal TV on top of your TV:

1. Open the large clip.
2. Open the small clip.
3. Rest the front clip against the front of your TV frame. At the same time, press the front clip against the front of your TV frame and the back clip against the back of your TV.
4. To make sure Portal TV is secure, press the back clip firmly against the back of your TV.

Set up your remote:

1. Remove the plastic battery tab on the back of your remote control.
2. Press Select, when prompted on-screen, to begin pairing the remote to Portal TV.

3. Follow the on-screen steps to finish setup.

Your Portal remote may require updating. This can take up to 5 minutes, depending on your connection. Make sure you don't press any buttons or remove the batteries while the update is happening.

Select your language and connect to Wi-Fi:

1. Select your language.
2. Connect to Wi-Fi by selecting your Wi-Fi network and entering your password. Select Continue to agree to download and install the latest Portal TV software. This can take about 15 minutes depending on your connection.
3. You may need to select **Restart Portal** to continue. If your Portal TV doesn't automatically restart, you may need to unplug and plug it back in.

Give your Portal TV a name and log in with Facebook or WhatsApp.

Follow the on-screen instructions to continue the setup process.

1. Give your Portal TV a name. Select an option from the menu or select **Custom...** to create a Custom Name.
2. Connect your Facebook or WhatsApp account:
3. Select **Facebook** or **WhatsApp**, then select **Continue** and follow the on-screen instructions.

How do I add or remove accounts on my Portal TV?

You can have up to 4 accounts linked to your Portal TV. The accounts you add must be Facebook friends with an account already connected to your Portal.

Only invite people you trust to have an account on your Portal TV. When you add an account to your Portal, that person becomes another authorized user on your Portal TV, and they'll be able to:

- See, hear, and delete all of your Portal TV voice interactions in Portal TV **Settings** or from their **Facebook Activity Log.**
- Make changes to voice interaction settings on your Portal TV, which will apply to your voice interactions.
- Use and change other settings on your Portal TV, which may apply across your Portal TV.
- Add accounts to, or remove accounts from, your Portal TV, which could include removing your account.
- View and access any information you use or access on your Portal TV, including the ability to view and call your contacts.

Also, when someone adds an account on your Portal TV, their Facebook friends and Messenger connections will become contacts on your Portal TV. If they add their WhatsApp account to your Portal TV, their WhatsApp contacts will also become contacts on your Portal TV. You will then be able to call their contacts and they will be able to call your contacts from Portal TV.

1. From **Home** on your Portal, select **Settings.**
2. Select **Accounts.**
3. Select **Add Account.**
4. Follow the on-screen instructions to confirm your Facebook account.
5. Select **Next.**
6. Select **Continue.**
7. Select **Log in with Facebook.**
8. Have the person you'd like to add follow the on-screen instruction to log in with their Facebook account.

To remove an account from your Portal:

1. From **Home** on your Portal, select **Settings.**
2. Select **Accounts.**
3. Select the account you'd like to remove.

4. Select **Remove Portal Account** and follow the on-screen instructions.

Notes:

- You can also remove your own account from your Portal TV from the **Security and Login** menu in your Facebook settings. If your Facebook account is deleted, deactivated or you change your Facebook password, your account will also be removed from your Portal TV.
- Anyone who uses your Portal TV, not just another owner, can view and call all contacts, manage favorites, see photos added to your Portal TV, and use third-party services connected to your Portal.
- Removing an account from your Portal TV will remove the contacts, photos and other data associated with that account, and will remove the account holder from certain connected third party apps.

- Removing all accounts that are connected to a Portal TV will automatically factory reset that Portal.
- If one of multiple account holders is removed from your Portal TV, call history on the Portal TV will remain, but it will no longer show that the removed account holder initiated a call.

How does calling work on Portal TV?

With Portal TV, you can make calls to and receive calls from your Facebook friends, Messenger connections and WhatsApp contacts. Portal TV calls can be received on Portal devices, the Messenger app on mobile phones or tablets, or WhatsApp on mobile phones. To call a WhatsApp contact from your Portal TV, the contact must have WhatsApp open or in standby mode on their mobile phone.

Making a call

1. From **Home** on your Portal TV, open the **Contacts** app. You can filter your contacts by **Favorites, Recents,** and **Messenger.** You can also **Search.** If you've connected your WhatsApp account to your Portal TV, you can also filter by **WhatsApp**.
2. Select a contact.
3. Select **Video** to start your call.

You can also use voice commands to make a call by saying: "Hey Portal, call [contact name]." For example, "Hey Portal, call John Doe."

Answering a call

If you have HDMI-CEC enabled on your TV and on Portal TV, when you receive an incoming call, Portal TV will not turn on your TV or switch the input until you've answered the call. If you don't have HDMI-CEC enabled or if your TV doesn't support HDMI-CEC, when you're receiving an incoming call you should first turn on your TV and switch to the correct input before answering a call.

To answer a call you can do things like:

- Select **Answer** to join the call.
- Press ⏯ on the Portal TV remote.
- Say "Hey Portal, answer."
- Press 🎤 on your Portal TV remote and say "Hey Portal, answer."

Ending a call

To end a call:

1. Press Select to expose the call menu.
2. Select **X** to end the call.

Call features

During a call you can do things like:

- Move around and talk hands-free. Portal's Smart Camera keeps you in-frame and Smart Sound enhances the voice of whoever is speaking while minimizing unwanted background noise.
- Turn your microphone or camera on or off.

- Add more friends to the call.
- Use **AR Effects** and **Story Time.**

How do I turn the camera and microphone off on my Portal TV?

To turn the camera and microphone off on Portal TV:

Press the camera and microphones on/off button on the side of your device. Once the button has been pressed, a red light on your device indicates that the camera and microphones are off. Keep in mind that pressing 🎤 on your Portal TV remote will continue to work, even when your microphone is turned off.

To turn the camera and microphones back on:

Press the camera and microphones on/off button on the side of your device.

To block the camera lens on Portal TV:

Use the integrated camera cover.

How do I make group calls on my Portal TV?

Group calls with Messenger connections:

With Portal TV, you can add up to 7 Messenger connections to a call for a total of 8 people, including yourself. You or other connections on your call can add any Facebook friends or Messenger connections to your call. You can't have both Messenger and WhatsApp users on the same call.

Group calls with WhatsApp contacts:

With Portal TV, you can add up to 3 WhatsApp contacts to a call for a total of 4 people, including yourself. You or other contacts on your call can add any WhatsApp contacts to your call. In order to call any WhatsApp contact from your Portal TV, the contact must have WhatsApp open or in standby mode on their mobile phone.

You can't have both Messenger and WhatsApp users on the same call.

To make a group call on your Portal TV:

1. Start a call with one of the contacts you'd like to join the group call.
2. During the call, press Select to expose the call menu.
3. Select and then select the contact you'd like to add to your call.

How do I use AR Effects during a call on my Portal TV?

You can use **AR Effects** like filters and masks during a call on your Portal TV. If you use **AR Effects,** they will only appear on the person who added the Effect. Shared Effects appear on everyone, but are only available when everyone on the call is using Portal.

To use AR Effects or Shared Effects during a call:

1. Press Select to expose the call menu.
2. Select and then select **Effects** or **Shared Effects.**
3. Select the Effect you'd like to try.

If Shared Effects don't appear during a call:

Make sure everyone on the call is using a Portal

How do I use Story Time on my Portal TV?

On Portal TV, **Story Time** allows you to share interactive stories with animations, music and **AR Effects** during a call or while you're using the **Story Time** app.

To use Story Time during a call:

1. Press Select to expose the call menu.
2. Select **Story Time.**

3. Select the story you'd like to share.

To stop Story Time during a call:

1. Press ⬅ on your Portal TV remote.
2. Next to **Story Time,** select **X.**

To use the Story Time app:

1. From **Home,** select the **Story Time** app.
2. Select the story you'd like to start.

Notes:

- Stories can take up to 45 seconds to load.
- To use the **Story Time** app, enable your microphone and camera.
- If you experience trouble loading a story or see a loading signal in the middle of a story, check your internet connection.
- Features, functionality, and content are subject to change or withdrawal at any time, may not be available in all areas or languages or may be restricted, may require enabled software or service activation, and

additional terms, conditions and/or charges may apply.

How do I connect or disconnect Alexa on my Portal TV?

To use Alexa on your Portal, you must connect an Amazon Alexa account to your Portal. You can connect to Alexa during the setup of your Portal, or from **Settings.**

To connect Alexa:

1. From **Home,** select **Settings.**
2. Select **Accounts.**
3. Select **Amazon Alexa** and follow the on-screen instructions to log in with your Amazon account or to disconnect Alexa.
4. Select **Continue.**
5. Select **Done.**

To deregister Alexa:

1. From **Home,** select **Settings.**
2. Select **Accounts.**
3. Select **Amazon Alexa.**
4. Select **Device Options.**
5. Select **Deregister.**
6. Select **YES.**

Notes:

- The Alexa account connected to Portal isn't linked to a particular Portal account. If one of multiple Portal accounts is removed from your Portal, the Alexa app will remain connected on the device.
- You can also disconnect Alexa by using the Alexa app.

How do I use my Portal TV remote?

Your Portal TV remote allows you to Select, navigate, go Home, go back, play, pause, "sleep," "wake," control the volume and control voice input.

Using your Portal TV remote:

- Press the center button to Select.
- Press up, down, right or left around the Select button to navigate.
- Press ⬅ to go back. The back button can also bring up additional functions during a call.
- Press ⌂ to go Home.
- Press ⏯ to play or pause.
- Press 🎤 for voice input, where available. Language selection will affect "Hey Portal" and other functionality.
- Press ⏻ to put your Portal TV in "sleep" mode or to "wake" your Portal TV. This will also turn the connected TV on or off if you have HDMI-CEC enabled.
- Press to control the volume.

Notes:

- If your Portal TV is connected to your TV, the volume buttons on your Portal TV remote will control the TV volume only.
- If your Portal TV is connected to your audio/video receiver (AV/R), the volume buttons on your Portal TV remote will control the AV/R volume only.

How do I connect my WhatsApp account to my Portal TV?

To connect your WhatsApp account to your Portal TV:

1. From **Home,** select **Settings.**
2. Select **Accounts.**
3. Select **[Your name].**
4. Select **Connect WhatsApp.** You may be asked to confirm your login to make changes.

5. Select the box next to **By checking, you agree to receive messages on WhatsApp,** then select **Continue.**
6. Read about how your WhatsApp info is managed on Portal, then select **Next.**
7. Follow the on-screen instructions. Make sure you have the latest version of WhatsApp downloaded to your mobile device.

How do I view regulatory information about my Portal TV?

To view your Portal's regulatory information:

1. From **Home,** select **Settings.**
2. Select **About.** From there you can select things like **Legal and Safety** and **Regulatory.**

How do I add or remove Favorites from my Portal TV?

To add someone to your favorites using Portal TV:

1. From **Home** on your Portal TV, select **Contacts**.
2. Select the contact you want to add to your favorites.
3. Select **Favorite**.

To remove someone from your favorites using Portal TV:

1. From **Home** on your Portal TV, select **Contacts**
2. Under **Favorites,** select the contact you'd like to remove.
3. Select **Favorited.**

To add someone to your favorites from the Portal app:

1. Open the Portal app on your mobile device.
2. Tap the Portal you'd like to manage.
3. Tap **Favorites.**
4. Tap **Add a Favorite.**

5. Tap the name of any contact and then tap **Add.**

To remove someone from your favorites from the Portal app:

1. Open the Portal app on your mobile device.
2. Tap the Portal you'd like to manage.
3. Tap **Favorites.**
4. Tap the contact you'd like to remove from favorites.
5. Tap next to **Favorite.**

How do I set up or change the Wi-Fi network on my Portal TV?

During the initial setup of your Portal TV, you'll choose and connect to a Wi-Fi network. You can change your Portal TV's Wi-Fi network at any time.

To change your Portal TV's Wi-Fi network:

1. From **Home** on your Portal TV, select **Settings.**
2. Select **General.**
3. Select **Wi-Fi.**
4. Select the network you'd like to connect to, enter your Wi-Fi password, and select **Join.**

If you don't see your Wi-Fi network listed, enter it manually.

To enter your Wi-Fi network manually:

1. From **Home,** select **Settings.**
2. Select **General.**
3. Select **Wi-Fi** and make sure Wi-Fi is enabled.
4. Select **Other Network...** and enter your Wi-Fi network name.
5. Select your Wi-Fi network's security method from the dropdown, enter your Wi-Fi password and select **Join.**

How do I put my Portal TV in "sleep" mode?

"Sleep" mode

You can put your Portal TV in "sleep" mode, which turns the display off, but allows your Portal TV to be woken up by voice commands, using the remote or receiving an incoming call. When your Portal TV is in sleep mode, it is still connected to Wi-Fi and its sensors are still active.

Putting your Portal TV in sleep mode

You can put your Portal in sleep mode manually by pressing ⏻ on your Portal TV remote.

Adjusting your display settings

Your Portal will go to sleep automatically when no motion is detected for a preset amount of time. You can adjust your display settings in **Settings > General > Display.**

How do I pair my Portal TV remote?

To begin using your Portal TV remote, you will need to pair your remote during setup.

To pair your Portal TV remote during setup:

1. Remove the plastic battery tab on the back of your remote control.
2. Press Select, when prompted on-screen, to begin pairing the remote to Portal TV.
3. Follow the on-screen steps to finish setup.

Your Portal remote may require updating. This can take up to 5 minutes, depending on your connection. Make sure you don't press any buttons or remove the batteries while the update is happening.

To pair your Portal TV remote after performing a factory reset:

Press and hold ⬅ and ⏵⏸ on your Portal TV remote at the same time for 3 seconds.

If you're having trouble pairing your Portal TV remote:

How do I pair my new Portal TV remote?

To pair your new remote, you'll have to factory reset your Portal TV:

1. Make sure your TV is turned on and you can see Portal's Home screen.

2. Unplug the power cord from the back of your Portal TV.

3. Press and hold the button on the right side of your Portal TV. At the same time, plug the power cord back into your Portal TV.

I'm having trouble with my Portal TV remote.

If you're having trouble pairing your Portal TV remote during setup:

- Press and hold ⬅ and ⏯ on your Portal TV remote at the same time for 3 seconds.
- Unplug your Portal TV, then plug it back in again.
- Perform a factory reset on your Portal TV and follow the on-screen instructions to pair your Portal TV remote.

If your Portal TV remote is unresponsive:

- Check to make sure the batteries have been loaded correctly.
- Try removing the batteries for a few minutes and then putting the batteries back into your Portal TV remote.
- Try replacing the batteries. Your Portal TV remote requires 2 AAA batteries.

- Unplug your Portal TV, then plug it back in again.
- Perform a factory reset.
- **If you're still experiencing issues with your Portal TV remote:**

How do I factory reset my Portal TV?

Resetting your Portal TV will set the device to its original factory settings and will disconnect any accounts, erase any preferences, local device data and or settings you've set on the device.

To perform a factory reset on your Portal TV using the Portal TV remote:

1. From **Home** on your Portal, select **Settings.**
2. Select **General.**
3. Scroll down and select **Factory Reset.**
4. Select **Reset** to complete a factory reset on your Portal.

To manually perform a factory reset on your Portal TV:

1. Unplug your Portal TV.
2. Press and hold the button on the side of your Portal TV while plugging your Portal TV back in at the same time. You will see a notification and countdown on your TV screen letting you know that your Portal TV will Factory Reset in 10 seconds.

How do I use Portal safely with kids in my home?

- Set a 12-digit pass code to keep your screen locked when it's not in use.
- Turn your microphone and camera off when you aren't using your Portal, or use the included camera cover.

How do I know if my contacts are available to call on my Portal?

Contacts that have a ●next to their name are recently active on their Portal, Messenger or Facebook. If someone has set to allow you to see when they're home on Portal, you'll see a when they're home and available to call.

What is Mic Drop on Portal TV?

Mic Drop is an in-call experience on Portal TV that lets you lip sync to song clips and perform them on an AR stage. Mic Drop is only available when making calls between one Portal TV and another Portal TV.

To use Mic Drop on Portal TV:

1. Start a call with another Portal TV.

2. During the call, press Select to expose the in-call menu.
3. Select 🎭.
4. Select **Mic Drop** and follow the on-screen instructions.

How do I control the camera during a call on my Portal TV?

During a call you can move around the room and talk freely while Portal TV's Smart Camera and Smart Sound adjust to keep you audible and in the frame. You can also adjust your camera to focus on one individual (**Spotlight**) during a call.

To turn on Spotlight during a call:

1. Press Select to expose the call menu.
2. Use the Portal TV remote navigation to choose the person you'd like to focus on in the call. When a white rectangle appears over their face, press select. The rectangle will turn green and you will see a notification

on your Portal TV display letting you know that **Spotlight is on.**

To turn Spotlight off during a call:

Use your Portal TV remote to navigate to and select 🗗 on your Portal TV display. You will see a notification on your Portal TV display letting you know that **Spotlight is off.**

To control your camera's self view during a call:

1. Press Select to expose the menu options.
2. Press up to navigate to your self view.
3. You can switch your display view by selecting ↗.

How do I hide a suggested or recent contact on Portal TV?

To hide a suggested or recent contact:

1. Select the suggested or recent contact you'd like to hide.
2. Select **More.**
3. Select **Hide Contact.** If you hide the contact, you won't be able to connect with them on Portal TV. You can unhide them later in **Settings > Privacy.**
4. Select **Hide.**

How do I create or edit a custom nickname on Portal TV?

To create or edit a custom nickname:

1. From **Home,** select **Contacts.**
2. Select the contact you'd like to rename.
3. Select **More.**
4. Select **Add Nickname.**
5. Add a custom nickname using the onscreen keyboard.

6. Select **Save.** You can now call the contact using their custom nickname by saying "Hey Portal, call [nickname]."

How do I change the Call Settings on my Portal TV?

Call Settings allow you to set when you receive incoming calls on Portal TV. You can select **Do Not Disturb,** which silences your calls and shows you as not active until 8AM. **Call Settings** can be uniquely set for each account on your Portal TV.

To change your Call Settings:

1. **From Home**, select **Settings.**
2. Select **General.**
3. Under Call Settings, select next to **Do Not Disturb.**

How do I call someone using their Facebook relationship name or nickname?

If you've added someone to the Family and Relationships section of your Facebook profile, you can call them on Portal using voice controls and your relationship name (or common synonyms for those names). Any relationship names on Facebook can be used.

For example, you can call your mother by saying either:

- "Hey Portal, call my mother."
- "Hey Portal, call Mom."

Notes:

- If you list a Facebook friend as your family member or that you're in a relationship with them, that person will be asked to confirm your relationship on Facebook.

- In order to use relationship names in voice commands, your relationship must be shared with your Facebook Friends or shared as Public to be associated with a contact on your Portal.
- You can also create or edit a custom nickname for your contacts on Portal.

Who can I call or receive calls from on Portal?

Making calls on Portal:

On Portal you can call the Facebook friends, Messenger connections and WhatsApp contacts of any accounts linked to your Portal. You can use your Portal to call friends located in any country where the Messenger app or WhatsApp are supported.

Receiving calls on Portal:

Currently, Portal calls can only be received from other Portal devices, from WhatsApp on mobile devices, from the Messenger app on mobile devices or tablets, from messenger.com or from facebook.com. Portal can't be called from Messenger Kids accounts or the Messenger Lite app.

Your Portal contacts:

Your Portal contacts are the Facebook friends, Messenger connections and WhatsApp contacts of all accounts linked to your Portal. If you share a Portal with others, all accounts that have been linked to your Portal will share contacts on Portal. Anyone who shares your Portal will have access to the contacts on the device and will be able to make and answer calls.

Viewing your Portal contacts:

From **Home** on your Portal, tap **Contacts.** From there, you can browse by **Suggested** contacts, **Recent** contacts or contacts by account type.

Why am I being asked to log in to my Portal again?

Reasons you may be asked to log in again include:

- You changed your Facebook password.
- Multiple accounts are logged in on your Portal and one of the accounts got logged out.
- Multiple accounts are logged in on your Portal and one of the accounts changed their Facebook password.
- There was a software update on your Portal.

To log back in to your Portal, follow the on-screen instructions.

Why do I have to log in with Facebook to view or edit certain settings on my Portal?

Some settings require you to confirm your Facebook login to make sure you are the one viewing or editing these settings on your Portal.

You can control this with the following options:

- If you have already confirmed your login status in **Settings** on your Portal and don't close the **Settings** menu, you won't be required to re-authenticate your status to access some settings for a short period of time.
- During your initial Portal setup or when accessing some settings on your Portal, selecting the checkbox next to **Don't ask me to confirm my login again** will allow you to access some settings without logging in again with Facebook.

Notes:

- Some settings will always require authentication, such as when new accounts are added to Portal.
- If you allow access to some settings without logging in again with Facebook, anyone who has access to your Portal will be able to view and edit those settings.

How do I change the language settings on my Portal TV?

To change the language settings on your Portal TV:

1. From **Home,** select **Settings.**
2. Select **General.**
3. Select **Language and Keyboard.**
4. Select **Device Language.**
5. Select any language.
6. Restart your Portal TV by unplugging it and plugging it back in.

How does HDMI-CEC work on Portal TV?

HDMI Consumer Electronics Control (HDMI-CEC) is a protocol on some TVs that you can turn on and off using your TV remote. When HDMI-CEC is turned on it allows devices like Portal TV to communicate with the TV it's connected to.

HDMI-CEC is also supported on Portal TV, and you can turn it on and off in **Settings** using your Portal TV remote. In order for HDMI-CEC to work properly, turn HDMI-CEC on in your Portal TV **Settings** and your TV settings.

When HDMI-CEC is turned on, your Portal TV can do things like:

- Turn your TV on and change the input source when you accept an incoming call on Portal TV.
- Turn your TV off when your Portal TV is not in use.

To turn HDMI-CEC on or off on your Portal TV:

1. From **Home,** select **Settings.**
2. Select **Remote.**
3. Select **TV and Receiver Control.** Next to **TV and Receiver Control** you can see if HDMI-CEC is **On** or **Off.** By default, HDMI-CEC will be turned **On.**

Notes:

- Not all devices support HDMI-CEC.
- Different TV manufacturers refer to HDMI-CEC by different names.

How do I control audio settings on my Portal TV?

In your Portal TV **Settings,** you can control things like **Portal Volume, Smart Sound Balance** and **Navigation sounds.**

Portal Volume adjusts the volume for call ringer, assistant responses, and camera and mic control. **Smart Sound Balance** adjusts volume levels between voices in a call and media you share in a call. **Navigation sounds** can be turned on or off.

To adjust your Portal Volume:

1. From **Home,** select **Settings.**
2. Select **General,** and then select **Audio.**
3. Select **Portal Volume,** then use the right navigation on your Portal TV remote to turn your **Portal Volume** up and the left navigation to turn your **Portal Volume** down.

To adjust your Smart Sound Balance:

1. From **Home,** select **Settings.**
2. Select **General,** and then select **Audio.**
3. Select **Smart Sound Balance.** Use the right navigation on your Portal TV remote to turn your **Smart Sound Balance** up and the left navigation to turn your **Smart**

Sound Balance down. The default setting for **Smart Sound Balance** is **+60% Call.**

To turn your Navigation sounds on or off:

1. From **Home,** select **Settings.**
2. Select **General,** and then select **Audio.**
3. Select next to **Navigation sounds** to turn **Navigation sounds** on or off.

How do I adjust the accessibility settings on my Portal TV?

To adjust accessibility settings on your Portal:

1. From **Home** on your Portal, select **Settings.**
2. Select **Accessibility** .

From here you can control and adjust:

- Font Size

- **High Contrast Text**
- **Vision Accessibility Options:** You can also enable or disable **Vision Accessibility Options** with your Portal TV remote by pressing ⬅ and ⌂ at the same time and holding them for 5 seconds.
- **Captions**

Note: The volume buttons on your Portal TV remote control the TV volume.

How do I update the software on my Portal?

Your Portal software will update automatically when connected to Wi-Fi and turned on. In order to make sure your Portal software updates automatically:

- Ensure your Portal is turned on and connected to Wi-Fi when leaving your Portal idle.

- Allow your Portal to remain idle for up to 3 hours to ensure it updates to the latest software version.

How do I connect my Portal to a TV, computer monitor or Ethernet?

Connecting to Ethernet, a TV or a computer monitor are beta features. Beta features might not always work as expected.

Connecting to Ethernet:

You can use a compatible adapter to connect your Portal to Ethernet.

Connecting to a TV or computer monitor:

You can use a compatible adapter and cable to connect your Portal to a TV or computer monitor. When connected, the Portal display will appear on the TV or computer monitor. Audio will still come from the Portal speakers.

Compatible adapters for USB-C to Ethernet include:

- Apple
- Belkin

Compatible adapters for USB-C to display port include:

- HuDieM: B07766TXQF
- TopGeek: B074MZV33N
- Uni: UNICHDMIF01

Compatible adapters for USB-C to HDMI include:

- CableCreation: CD0001
- Mokin: 4328314362
- Anker: AK-A8306041
- TopGeek: B074MZV33N
- Monoprice: 113235
- Cable Matters: FBA_201018-BLK
- Lenovo: C103
- AmazonBasics: L6LUD005-CS-R
- Choetech: HUB-H06

- HuDieM: B07766TXQF

Notes:

- USB-C hubs and splitters are not supported.
- Video and Ethernet cannot be used at the same time.
- Apple USB-C to HDMI adapters are not compatible.

How do I set up or change the Wi-Fi network on my Portal TV?

During the initial setup of your Portal TV, you'll choose and connect to a Wi-Fi network. You can change your Portal TV's Wi-Fi network at any time.

To change your Portal TV's Wi-Fi network:

1. From **Home** on your Portal TV, select **Settings.**
2. Select **General.**

3. Select **Wi-Fi.**
4. Select the network you'd like to connect to, enter your Wi-Fi password, and select **Join.**

If you don't see your Wi-Fi network listed, enter it manually.

To enter your Wi-Fi network manually:

1. From **Home,** select **Settings.**
2. Select **General.**
3. Select **Wi-Fi** and make sure Wi-Fi is enabled.
4. Select **Other Network...** and enter your Wi-Fi network name.
5. Select your Wi-Fi network's security method from the dropdown, enter your Wi-Fi password and select **Join.**

How do I adjust Superframe settings on my Portal TV?

To adjust Superframe settings on your Portal TV:

1. From **Home**, select **Settings.**
2. Select **Superframe.**

From here, you can control and adjust things like:

- **Transition Speed:** Adjust the frequency that Superframe rotates through pictures and videos.
- **Photos:** Manage the photos that will display on Superframe.
- **Hidden Photos:** Manage your hidden Superframe photos and videos.

How do I add or remove photos from Superframe on my Portal TV?

You can select which Facebook photos you'd like to add to Superframe. You can also remove or hide photos at any time.

To add or remove Facebook photos or albums from Superframe:

1. From **Home** on your Portal TV, select **Settings**.
2. Select **Superframe**.
3. Select **Photos**.
4. Select ⬤ next to any albums you'd like to add to or remove from Superframe.

To hide a photo from Superframe:

1. When Superframe is displayed on your Portal TV and you see a photo you'd like to hide, press Down on your Portal TV remote navigation.
2. Select **Hide**.

To unhide photos you've hidden on Superframe:

1. From **Home** on your Portal TV, select **Settings**.
2. Select **Superframe**.

3. Select **Hidden Photos**. You may need to confirm your login to make changes.
4. Select the photo you'd like to unhide.
5. Select **Unhide Photo**.
6. Select **Show**.

If you remove a photo from Facebook_that was previously visible on Superframe, it will no longer appear on Portal.

How do I manage Superframe photos using the Portal app?

If you're managing Superframe photos using the Portal app:

- You can upload up to 20 photos to Superframe at once.
- You cannot add or delete photos when an upload is in progress.
- Photos you upload from the camera roll will only be displayed in the Portal app and on your household device.

To manage Superframe photos using the Portal app:

1. Open the app and tap your Portal.
2. Tap **Superframe.**
3. Tap ⬤ next to any albums you'd like to add to or remove from Superframe.

To create an album in Superframe using the Portal app:

1. Open the app and tap your Portal.
2. Tap **Create Album.**
3. Tap **Add Photos,** select photos from your camera roll, then tap **Add**.
4. Tap ⬤ next to **Display in Superframe.**

How can I add photos to Superframe that I don't want to share on Facebook?

You can add any of your Facebook photo albums to Superframe on Portal, including albums you've set to **Only Me** under your photo privacy settings.

Notes:

- Friends tagged in **Only Me** posts will receive a Facebook notification and will be able to see the post.
- Facebook may suggest tags for photos, even when set to **Only Me**, so make sure to manually remove all tags before finalizing and posting your album if you don't want the photos seen outside your Portal.

How do I edit the privacy settings for my photo albums on Facebook?

To edit the privacy settings for your photo albums:

1. From your News Feed, click your name in the top left to go to your profile.
2. Click **Photos**, then click **Albums**.

3. Click the album you want to change the privacy settings for.
4. Click **Edit** in the top right.
5. Click ▾below **Privacy** to control who can see your album.

Only the person who posted an album can change its privacy settings.

How do I manage the apps on my Portal TV?

To add apps to your Portal TV Home screen:

1. Select **Portal Apps.**
2. Select the app you'd like to add to your Portal TV Home screen.
3. Select **Get.**

To move apps on your Portal TV Home screen:

1. Using the Portal TV remote, press and hold Select on the app you'd like to move around on your Portal TV Home screen.
2. Use the right, left, up and down navigation on your Portal TV remote to move the app.
3. Press Select to place the app in your desired location.

To remove apps from your Portal TV Home screen:

1. Using the Portal TV remote, press and hold Select on the app you'd like to remove from your Portal TV Home screen.
2. Press ⏵⏸.
3. Select **Delete.**

Note: Removing an app from your Portal TV Home screen doesn't disconnect your credentials or subscriptions from the app you have removed. It also doesn't remove any of your data associated with the app.

How do I connect my Spotify, Pandora or iHeartRadio accounts to Portal TV?

You can connect and play music through several streaming services on your Portal TV, including Spotify, Pandora and iHeartRadio in some countries. App availability may differ based on the country where you use Portal TV.

Spotify

To use Spotify, select **Spotify** from **Home** on your Portal TV. A Spotify Premium account isn't required to use Spotify on Portal TV.

To connect your Spotify Premium account:

1. From **Home** on your Portal TV, select **Spotify**.
2. Select **Log In.**
3. Follow the on-screen instructions to connect your Spotify account.

Pandora

To connect a Pandora account, you can use a Pandora, Pandora Plus, or Pandora Premium account. Pandora is only currently available if you use Portal TV in the US.

To connect Pandora:

1. From **Home** on your Portal, select **Pandora**.
2. Select **Connect Pandora**.
3. Select **I have a Pandora account.**
4. Use the on-screen keyboard to enter your email address and password.
5. Select **Log In.**

iHeartRadio

To use iHeartRadio, select **iHeartRadio** from **Home** on your Portal TV. An iHeartRadio account isn't required to use iHeartRadio on Portal TV. iHeartRadio is only currently available if you use Portal TV in the US.

Notes:

- You can disconnect your third-party accounts from Portal in **Settings** through **Accounts** by selecting **Disconnect** next to the account you want to disconnect.
- If an account that was connected to Spotify or Pandora is removed from your Portal TV, the third-party service will be disconnected from the device

How do I connect Bluetooth devices to my Portal TV?

To connect a Bluetooth device to your Portal TV:

1. From **Home** on your Portal TV, select **Settings.**
2. Select **General.**
3. Select **Bluetooth.**
4. Select **Pair a Device.** Make sure your device is in Bluetooth pairing mode.

5. Select your Bluetooth device from the available devices list on your Portal TV or select your Portal TV from the Bluetooth settings on your device to pair the device.

Note that not all Bluetooth devices will be available to connect to your Portal TV.

To unpair a Bluetooth device from your Portal TV:

1. From **Home** on your Portal TV, select **Settings.**
2. Select **General.**
3. Select **Bluetooth.**
4. Select the device you'd like to unpair from the list of Available Devices.
5. Select **Unpair.**
6. Select **Unpair.**

Can I go live on Facebook using my Portal?

Facebook Live is supported on Portal, Portal Mini and Portal+. Facebook Live isn't supported on Portal TV.

To use Facebook Live on Portal, Portal Mini and Portal+:

1. From **Home**, tap to open the **Facebook Live** app. You can choose your audience and **Add a description.**
2. Tap **Start Live Video.**

When you go live on Facebook, your live broadcast will share in stories and as a post.

During a live broadcast on Portal, you can view things like:

- How many people are watching
- Comments
- Reactions

How do I set up a passcode for my Portal TV?

You can set a 4-12 digit passcode to keep your Portal TV screen locked when it's not in use. The passcode will be required to return to Home from Superframe.

While your Portal TV is locked, you won't be able to add additional contacts to a call.

To set your Portal TV passcode:

1. From **Home** on your Portal TV, select **Settings.**
2. Select **Privacy,** then select **Passcode.**
3. Enter a 4-12 digit passcode for your device, then select ✓.
4. Re-enter your 4-12 digit passcode and select ✓ to confirm your passcode.
5. Select **OK.**

What do the lights on my Portal TV mean?

The lights on your Portal TV are used to indicate when different parts of your Portal TV are in use or not in use:

- **Green light:** A green light indicates when the camera is in use for video. When the green light is on, it may mean that the microphones may also be in use for some applications.
- **White light:** A white light indicates when the microphones are in use by audio-only applications, like audio calls or voice interactions. A white light will also appear when your Portal TV is being plugged in and powered up, when alarms and timers are going off, and for incoming calls.
- **Red light:** A red light indicates when both the camera and microphone are off.

How do I remove an account from Portal remotely?

You can remove your account from Portal from your Facebook settings.

To remove your account remotely:

1. Go to your Facebook settings.
2. Under **Your Active Portals,** select **Remove Yourself** next to the Portal you'd like to be removed from.

Does Portal have parental controls?

Portal lets you set a 4-12 digit passcode so only you and the people you give the passcode to have access to the device.

In addition:

- Portal does not support Messenger Kids and calls cannot be made to or from Messenger Kids accounts on Portal.

- You must have an active Facebook account and therefore be 13 years of age or older to log into Portal.

How do I take care of my Portal?

To take care of your Portal, follow these tips:

Picking a location

- Set up your Portal on a flat, stable surface where it's not likely to tip or fall.
- Set up and keep your Portal indoors in a well-ventilated, climate-controlled location. Your Portal may get warm during use, which is normal.
- Keep your Portal and its cord away from food, water or other liquids.
- Keep your Portal and its cord away from sources of heat like stoves, ovens or radiators.

Cord care

- When setting up Portal, plug the cord into the device first, then into an appropriate outlet.
- Arrange the cord so it's out of reach for children and pets, and no one will trip on it.
- Shut down and unplug your Portal before moving it.
- Unplug your Portal's cord from the outlet first, then from the device.
- Only use the included power cord with your Portal.

Cleaning your Portal:

- Use a clean, soft dry cloth to clean the screen and outside of your Portal.
- Only clean the outside of your Portal. Don't attempt to open your Portal or to clean inside any ventilation or other openings.
- Don't use compressed air to clean your Portal.
- Don't use abrasive or harsh chemicals when cleaning your Portal.

What information is collected for "Hey Portal"?

When Portal hears the wake word, "Hey Portal," it will start to record your voice interaction and create a computer-generated transcription of the recording. Like other voice assistants, when Portal is activated, it will also pick up other sounds in the immediate area beyond just the voice command - this may include ambient noise or nearby background conversations.

A voice command is something you ask Portal to do, such as "Hey Portal, call Mom" or "Hey Portal, what's the weather today?" Ambient noise or background conversation is any conversation or noise that happens in the background when you say a voice command that gets picked up by Portal. And a "false wake" recording is when Portal mistakenly hears the wake word and starts to record. When Portal is recording, you'll see a visual confirmation at the bottom of the screen. As Portal improves over time, it will get better at identifying and reducing the number of "false wakes," so you can have a better "Hey Portal" experience.

How does "Hey Portal" work with other voice services?

"Hey Portal" works independently from other voice services such as Amazon Alexa. If you activate Alexa on Portal and use the "Alexa" wake word, Amazon will process that request independently. Use of Alexa or any other third party voice services on Portal is subject to the terms and policies of those other services, not the terms and policies of Facebook and its products. Facebook doesn't collect voice interactions processed by a third party voice service.

How long do you keep my "Hey Portal" voice interactions?

Stored "Hey Portal" voice interactions are kept on Facebook servers for up to 3 years. We delete "false wakes" within 90 days of detection. When we delete voice interactions, they will no longer appear in your Portal Settings or Facebook Activity Log and will be deleted from our systems and no longer used as part of our human review or machine processes. You can always delete your "Hey Portal" voice interactions in Portal Settings or your Facebook Activity Log. Alternatively, you can turn off storage of your "Hey Portal" voice interactions in Portal Settings.

Can other people using my Portal see and access my voice interactions and settings?

Portal can be shared among multiple owners. If your Portal is shared, then all "Hey Portal" voice interactions and settings for that device will be accessible to you and the other owners. This means that other owners with whom you share your Portal will be able to see, hear and delete your voice interactions. Those people will also be able to turn off storage of "Hey Portal" voice interactions. If an owner is removed from your Portal, that person will no longer be able to perform these actions.

Do you share my 'Hey Portal' voice requests with anyone else?

Some third party apps or services on Portal, like Spotify, will respond to your "Hey Portal" voice commands. In order for this to work, Portal sends a text version of your "Hey Portal" voice command to the third party providing that app or service.

How do you use my 'Hey Portal' voice interactions?

"Hey Portal" voice interactions are used in a few different ways. Primarily, they are used to process and carry out your voice command. When you say "Hey Portal," your voice command is sent to Facebook's servers in real-time to process and respond to your request. We use stored "Hey Portal" voice interactions to help make our voice services get smarter, more accurate and better for everyone. We use a combination of human review and machine processes to troubleshoot and train our speech recognition systems. Lastly, we use "Hey Portal" voice commands to promote safety and integrity, and to help keep people safe on and off Facebook products

Does Portal record all of my conversations? How do I know when Portal is recording?

Portal only makes a recording when it hears the wake word, "Hey Portal." When Portal activates you will see a visual confirmation at the bottom of the screen. Additionally, you can have Portal play a beginning and ending sound when it processes a

"Hey Portal" voice interaction. You can turn this on in Portal **Settings** > **Privacy**.

How does "Hey Portal" work?

"Hey Portal" is a wake word that lets you use your Portal hands-free. If available to you, simply say "Hey Portal" when you want Portal to start a video call, check the weather or respond to other commands. Portal activates when it hears "Hey Portal" and gives you a visual confirmation at the bottom of the screen. When your Portal hears the wake word, it will start to record your voice interaction and send it to Facebook servers in real-time to respond to your request. When you turn Portal's microphone off, Portal won't listen for the wake word, and voice control will be disabled.

How do I control how Portal handles my voice interactions?

Portal offers clear and simple settings to control your voice interactions. You can choose to turn off storage of your "Hey Portal" voice interactions in Portal Settings. Even if you turn off storage, you can still use "Hey Portal" but the feature may not work as well. When storage is turned off, we won't keep recordings or transcripts of your voice interactions, which means you won't be able to view, hear or delete them. And we won't use those voice interactions to improve our voice services and they won't be reviewed by people. We'll still log system activity, such as the timestamp for when a voice interaction was made and the general category of the voice interaction. For example, if you said, "Hey Portal, what's the weather in Seattle?," we would simply categorize your question as "get weather." Any "Hey Portal" voice interactions made before you turned off storage will still be stored. You can easily view, hear and delete your "Hey Portal" voice interactions and transcriptions in Portal Settings or your Facebook Activity Log.

How do I use voice interactions with my Portal?

"Hey Portal" and Alexa are built into your Portal for hands-free control. In order to enable Alexa on your Portal, one of the accounts linked to your device must sign in to their Amazon account.

You can use "Hey Portal" to control things like:

- Calling.
- Weather.
- Time.
- Brightness control.
- Video control.
- Using camera Effects.

You can use Alexa to control things like:

- Playing music through music services connected to your Amazon account.
- Settings alarms or timers.
- Shopping and creating to-do lists.

- Some Alexa-supported features, like controlling smart-home devices.

For example:

- Set an alarm by saying, "Alexa, set an alarm."
- Start a video call by saying, "Hey Portal, call [contact name]" or "Hey Portal, call [Relationship Name]."
- Hear the local weather, birthdays, events and news by saying, "Hey Portal, good morning."

Notes:

- Your Portal's microphone must be turned on to use voice controls.
- Some Alexa features are not currently supported on Portal. This includes features like calling, drop in, announcements, messaging and photos.

How do I add a family member to my About page on Facebook?

To add a family member to your About page:

1. Go to your profile and click **About**.
2. Click **Family and Relationships**, then click **Add a family member**.
3. Enter the name of your family member and select your relationship.
4. Select an audience for your post and click **Save Changes**.

Note: If you list a Facebook friend as your family member, that person will be asked to confirm your relationship.

How do I change my relationship status on Facebook?

To add or edit your relationship status:

1. From your News Feed, click your name in the top left.
2. Click **About**, then **Family and Relationships** in the left column.
3. Click **Add your relationship status** or hover over your relationship and click **Edit**.

4. Choose your relationship status from the dropdown menu. Depending on your status, you may also have the option to add the name of the person you're in a relationship with and your anniversary.
5. Use the audience selector to choose who you wants to share this with.
6. Click **Save Changes**.

You can also add your relationship status as a life event on your profile.

Note: You can only list someone in your relationship status if you're friends with that person. That person also needs to confirm that you're in a relationship together before they're listed in your relationship status.

Hey Portal' and Alexa don't understand me.

If "Hey Portal" and Alexa have trouble understanding you:

- Make sure your Portal's microphone is turned on.
- Make sure your camera cover is not covering your Portal's microphone.
- Speak towards your Portal and move closer if necessary.
- Check to see if "Hey Portal" is available to you.

Printed in Great Britain
by Amazon